WELCOME
To The World Of You!

In this guided journal, you will learn self-empowerment, as you explore your strengths and weaknesses using creativity, self-reflection and self-love

There is no right or wrong way to complete this book.

Celebrate your uniqueness!

Start at the beginning, middle or end of the book; where you want to start your journaling is up to you!

See how amazing you really are.

Feel free to be honest when writing down your feelings, thoughts and questions!

About Me

I am curious about:

_____

_____

_____

What I like about me:

_____

_____

_____

Something I want to learn:

_____

_____

_____

What I am good at:

_____

_____

_____

Remember: you're the greatest!
May your life be as precious as 'you' are.

I help others by:

_____

_____

_____

Challenges
I've overcome:

_____

_____

_____

Things I am
good at:

_____

_____

_____

Things that are
important to me
in my life:

_____

_____

_____

People I Care About

Write the names of people
you care about in the hearts.

My Family

Draw or write your family members and fun memories you've shared with them in the picture frames.

Tell someone in your family that you love them today!

About Me

I am happy when... _____

_____

I am proud of... _____

_____

I am good at... _____

_____

Sometimes I worry about... _____

_____

It makes me sad when... _____

_____

What makes you a good friend?

_____

_____

_____

What is one thing you would like
to hear from a friend?

_____

_____

_____

How do you show your friends
that you care about them?

_____

_____

_____

What do you appreciate the most about your
friends or family?

_____

_____

The greatest person in your life is you.
List two positive beliefs you have
about yourself on the signs.

Remember to tell yourself...

I am
smart

I am
pretty

I am
proud
to be me

I am
loved

I am
special

My Story

What would the cover to the story of your life look like?

Remember the good memories of the
past, and look forward to your bright future!

Write a story about your past, present and future self.
Feel free to include your interests, hopes, fears and dreams.

My past self
_____
_____
_____
_____
_____

My present self
_____
_____
_____
_____
_____

My future self
_____
_____
_____
_____

I Am Grateful

Three people I am grateful for in my life:

One kind thing someone has done for me:

_____

_____

_____

One experience I am grateful for:

Three activities I enjoy:

Three things that make me smile:

_____

_____

_____

Thank You Notes

To _____

thank you

for

_____
_____
_____

To _____

thank you...

for

_____
_____
_____

When you take the time to thank the people in your life, it can make you and the people around you feel appreciated. Who are you grateful for?

My Award

Draw or write something you've accomplished
this year that makes you proud.

With hard work, courage and determination,
you can accomplish anything you set your mind to!

My Future Award

If you believe it, you can achieve it!

Draw or write one thing that you want to accomplish.

Draw Your Beautiful Self

In this world, there is only one you.
Draw your unique self below.

Believe In Yourself

Positive thinking can help positively shape your life and the world around you.

What have you accomplished by believing in yourself?

_____   _____
_____   _____

No matter what others think, it is important to always believe in yourself.

Be your own best friend

Don't put yourself down

Respect yourself

Recognize your strengths

Have faith in your abilities

Negative Beliefs

Negative self talk is not always true.
They are open to question.

Think ...

What negative thoughts about yourself do you have? Why might you be
thinking this way? Why might these negative beliefs not be true?

Write negative beliefs you
have about yourself on the lines below.

Write reasons why these negative
beliefs may not be true.

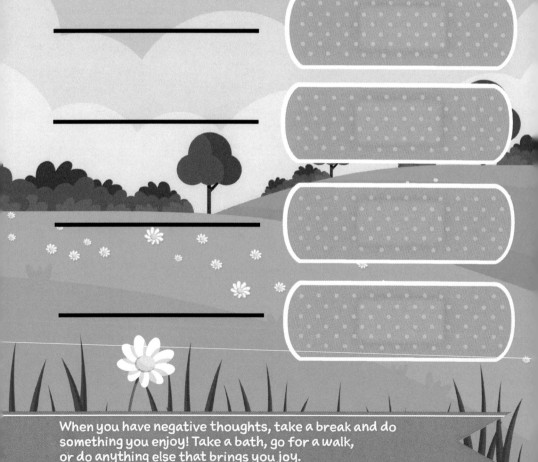

When you have negative thoughts, take a break and do
something you enjoy! Take a bath, go for a walk,
or do anything else that brings you joy.

Remind Yourself

How are you feeling today?
What emotions are you feeling right now?

What emotion are you feeling?

_____

_____

Why do you think you feel this way right now?

_____

_____

What do you usually do when you feel this way?

_____

_____

What emotion are you feeling?

_____

_____

Why do you think you feel this way right now?

_____

_____

What do you usually do when you feel this way?

_____

_____

It's natural and healthy to feel angry or worried. All feelings are ok!

My Worry

Write 3 things that make the worry grow larger.

Draw one thing that you worry about in the box below.

Write 3 things that help the worry to go away.

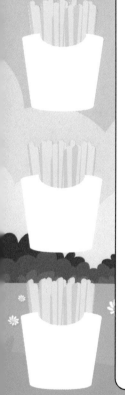

Try to find healthy ways to cope with your worries. Try talking with your friends or family about your worries, or taking time to do an activity you enjoy.

What I Am Grateful For

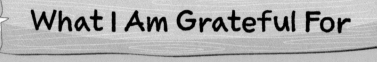

Write one thing you are grateful for on each leaf of the tree.

My Positive Thoughts

Color in the flower for each positive thought you have.

I am open to
learn new things

My efforts
pay off

I can
make a difference

I think positively

I have courage

I accept
who I am

My mistakes
help me grow

It's ok not to
know everything

I can do
hard things

I like myself

I am loved

I walk through
my fears
with confidence

Take a moment each day to think
positively about yourself.

Yours Truly

Imagine you are meeting someone for the first time.
What are three things about yourself that they should know?

1. _____

2. _____

3. _____

What is one thing that I am looking forward to?

_____

Who am I grateful to have in my life?

_____

What is my favorite memory?

_____

Keep Being You!

Color the food that best answers the question beside it.
Donuts are "Yes", French fries are "No",
and pizza slices are "Sometimes."

	Yes	No	Sometimes

I am polite and respectful towards my parents and teachers.

I can recognize and express my emotions, without losing control of them.

I try to see the bright side in every situation.

I don't give up on hard tasks.

I consider the feelings of my friends & family.

I can keep calm when things don't go my way.

I know when to put my phone or tablet down.

Checking Up With Myself

	Yes	No
I believe in myself		
I make wise choices		
Everything will be ok		
I think positive thoughts		
I can be a leader		
I like who I am		
I can handle criticism		
I trust myself		
I am happy to be me		
I love myself		
I am not afraid to try new things		
I put effort into everything I do.		

Making Smart Choices

My Adventure

Imagine you are on your dream trip to anywhere in the world. What would your dream trip look like? Where would you go? What would your postcard say? Who would you send it to?

Let's go on a
ADVENTURE

POSTCARD

to:

from:

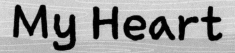

My Heart

Take a deep breath, and close your eyes.
Take a moment to listen to your heart;
what is your heart telling you?

Remember, the answer to many of life's problems comes
from within yourself. All of your thoughts, feelings and
emotions have a purpose, so it is important to keep track
of how you truly feel inside and what is best
for you when making choices.

Practice self-love every day.
Always remind yourself to love yourself.

Me Time

I want to be a:

_____

_____

_____

My least favorite things are:

_____

_____

_____

A time I made someone happy:

_____

_____

_____

What brings me most joy:

_____

_____

_____

What's Your Mood?

Draw a time where you were in a good mood.

What were you doing?

_____

_____

_____

What were you doing?

_____

_____

_____

Draw a time where you were in a bad mood.

It's okay to have bad moods, as long as you remember that bad moods will always pass and good moods will always return with time.

My Message

If you were leaving a message in a time capsule
for someone ten years in the future to find, what would you say?

My Feelings

Do you ever feel any of these emotions?
Write something that made you feel each emotion in the cookie.

worry

Mad

Excited

Brave

Happy

Upset

Superhero Advice

It's OK to make mistakes

Be Flexible

TURN OFF THE TV

Respect yourself

Be Positive

BE KIND TO OTHERS

Help someone who needs assistance.

Be your own #1 fan

KEEP THE PEACE

Be grateful for the things that you have

Listen to your heart!

Believe in yourself

Be grateful for the things that you have.

FOLLOW RULE

Try new thing

It's okay to no always win.

Think Positive Thoughts!

Supergirl

If you were a superhero, what would you look like?
What superpowers would you have?

I Like Me

Write 3 things you like about yourself on the lucky coins.

My Talents

Write your personal strengths and skills on the peacock feathers.

My Present

Draw a picture or write about what your dream present to yourself would be.

My Drawing

Use your imagination
to finish the drawing.

Color in the things that make you worried.

Family Problems

School

Fights with Friends

Not Fitting In

Something Bad Happening

Doing Poorly on Tests

Bullying

Monsters and the Dark

Practice accepting and releasing your worries by using visualization.
1-Sit down, close your eyes, and take three deep breaths in through your nose, and out through your mouth.
2-Notice your thoughts. Try not to judge them as good thoughts or bad thoughts. Let them come and go.
3-Imagine a glowing ball of light over your head.
Feel compassion for yourself, and feel the light and warmth enter your body.

My Feelings

Write a time when you have felt each emotion listed below on the unicorn's mane.

Upset

Mad

Excited

Brave

Lonely

Peaceful

My Worry Shield

Draw pictures of your interests, hobbies, and anything else that represents you on the shield.

WARRIOR

Name ————————————

Worries can grow stronger and stronger as the thoughts in your head feed your fear. Remember: your positive thoughts are more powerful then you realize.

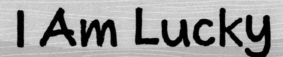

I Am Lucky

Write things that make you feel lucky on the balloons.

Remember: being lucky is not always about the gifts you get or the things you own.

Luck is often in the simple things in life, like petting your pet or getting a warm hug.

Focus on loving the things you already have.

Moments I want to relive:

Moments I look forward to:

Feeling grateful for
the past and hopeful
for the future is key
to happiness.

My Anger

It is normal and healthy to feel angry from time to time.
Draw a picture of what you look like or feel like when you're angry.

What do you say when you're angry?

When you are angry, how do you help yourself calm down and feel better?

My Strengths

Color the ones that apply to you.

Creativity

Curiosity

Leadership

Wisdom

Kindness

Fairness

Honesty

Forgiveness

Humor

Patience

Cooperation

Best Mistakes

Mistakes I've made:

How I learned and improved from my mistake:

Mistakes help you develop problem solving skills

♥ *Mistakes build character* ♥

Mistakes helps you understand what does not work

Share a story about when you overcame an obstacle in your life.

How has your life improved in the last week/month/year?

What helps you feel better when you're in a bad mood?

What is your favorite way to help other people in your daily life? Why?

I Am Unique

If you could be any person or animal for a day, who or what would you choose, and why?

What is one thing you wish you could spend more time doing? Why?

What qualities make for a good friend?

What is one thing you'd like to hear from your teacher/parent/friend?

I Am Unique

How would you like to help the world?

World
Peace Day!

If you could create the perfect imaginary friend, what would they be like?

if you were going to start a business or invent a product, what would it be?

What's the most beautiful thing you have seen today/yesterday/this week?

Going For It

Write five things you would like to do
that make you afraid on the ice cream scoops.

Alone Time

Write three things you like to do by yourself

#1

#2

#3

Made in the USA
Monee, IL
29 August 2020

40327264R00033